An Interactive, Integrated, Interdependent, Individualized Math Unit, Gr. 2-5

Money

by
Todd Daubert
Pauline Nelson

©1995

ECS
Learning Systems
INC.

Printed in the U.S.A.

ECS Learning Systems, Inc.
P.O. Box 791437
San Antonio, Texas 78279-1437

Editor: Jennifer Knoblock
Page Layout & Graphics: Lisa Avitia
Cover/Book Design: Educational Media Services
Art on pages 49, 72, 79, 80, 83, 84 by Corel GALLERY

ISBN 1-57022-045-X

Table of Contents

Table of Contents

INTRODUCTION

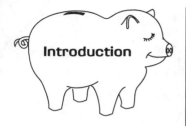

Welcome!

Today's math classroom is filled with students who:

- possess a wide range of abilities and learning styles
- have a need for enrichment and remediation
- have a need for time to work with teachers one-on-one or in small groups
- need to have their skills continuously assessed

Add to that:

- the National Council of Teachers of Mathematics (NCTM) broadening our understanding of the math curriculum (more than just computation)
- businesses calling for students who are self-motivated thinkers
- communities insisting that students be held accountable for basic skills
- children needing to experience a concept in a variety of ways in order to learn it

No matter which philosophy we hold or how our classroom is set up, the above realities are true for all teachers. Faced with those realities, we can choose to do nothing and allow everybody's needs to overwhelm us; we can choose to try many approaches in hopes that something will meet someone's needs; or we can stand alongside colleagues who have found success in the areas we all struggle with.

We invite you to share in the success we have found, and it is our hope that this book brings success to your classroom.

The purpose of this math learning guide is not radical educational reform. It is survival in the face of today's educational realities. It draws from the disciplines of language arts, science, geography, and the fine arts to teach a math concept. It combines many different approaches to the same concept. It combines direct instruction with student choice. It individualizes learning for students. It utilizes worksheets as well as learning centers. It allows children to work individually and cooperatively.

This learning guide was written by teachers who face the same realities that you face, and who believe that there is strength in combining the best of many different teaching styles. This guide is an attempt to meet the reality of today's needs, especially the needs of you and your students.

You need time to:

- assess students
- teach individual skill levels
- enrich students
- address individual learning styles

Your students need time to:

- experience a concept in many different ways
- learn to work independently and manage time
- excel in their learning styles
- learn basic and high-level skills
- problem solve
- work cooperatively with other students
- receive individual instruction from the teacher
- feel control over their own learning
- learn to make wise choices
- be successful

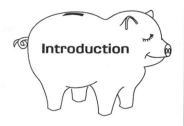

How to Use This Book

Ten Steps to Success

Following the simple steps provided in this teaching guide will allow you to implement the money unit into any classroom.

Student Activities

This collection of integrated activities is intended to guide your students through the entire learning experience. It is more of an activity journal than a workbook because it is intended to interact directly with the prepared activities that you choose and set up in your classroom. It contains a built-in time and activity management system in the form of a checklist and contract. It truly places the responsibility for organization and time management in the hands of your students.

Details, Details, Details

This section provides you with the details behind the ten steps that will ensure your success before, during, and after the learning experience. Specific guidance is provided in the following areas:

- preparing yourself, your classroom, your students and their parents
- teaching time management and work evaluation
- instruction, assessment, and skill grouping

Unit Overview Chart

Objective	Student Activity
Analyzing Data	Clean Up Your Act Money Talks Can You Put a Price on It? Get Rich Quick Pick a Pocket Ready, Set, Drip!
Arts/Crafts/Creativity	Coin Rubbings Design a Fast Food Park Get Rich Quick It Pays to Advertise It's in the Bag Making Faces Forgery! Papier-Mâché Bank Writing About Money
Coin Recognition	Warm-Ups Class Shop Coin Rubbings Heads or Tails Inflation! Money Games Pick a Pocket Take a Handful
Computation	All Change! Cheap! Cheaper! Cheapest! Class Shop Coin Rubbings Collect a Dollar Coupon Math Design a Fast Food Park Get Rich Quick Inflation! Making Faces Money Games Problem Solving Shop 'Til You Drop Take a Handful Wishing on a Star
Conducting a Survey	Can You Put a Price on It? Heads or Tails Money Talks

Unit Overview Chart

Objective	Student Activity
Cooperative Learning	Class Shop Collect a Dollar Get Rich Quick Inflation! Money Games Money Mania
Creative Problem Solving	All Change! Class Shop Coupon Math Design a Fast Food Park Get Rich Quick It's in the Bag Problem Solving Shop 'Til You Drop
Creative Writing	It Pays to Advertise Writing About Money
Cultural Awareness	All That Glitters Is Not Gold Money Research
Dramatic Play	Class Shop It's in the Bag
Experimenting	Clean Up Your Act Ready, Set, Drip!
Gathering Data	All That Glitters Is Not Gold Can You Put a Price on It? Clean Up Your Act Get Rich Quick Heads or Tails Money Research Money Talks Pick a Pocket Ready, Set, Drip!
Language Skills	All That Glitters Is Not Gold Class Shop Collect a Dollar Get Rich Quick It Pays to Advertise Money Games Shop 'Til You Drop

Unit Overview Chart

Objective	Student Activity
Making Change	Class Shop Collect a Dollar Money Games Problem Solving Shop 'Til You Drop
Map Skills	All That Glitters Is Not Gold Design a Fast Food Park Money Research Where Are the Federal Reserve Banks?
Observation	Warm-Ups Clean Up Your Act Coin Rubbings Heads or Tails It Pays to Advertise Ready, Set, Drip!
Predicting	Clean Up Your Act Heads or Tails Ready, Set, Drip!
"Real-life" Skills	Cheap! Cheaper! Cheapest! Class Shop Coupon Math Get Rich Quick Shop 'Til You Drop
Recording Data	Warm-Ups Can You Put a Price on It? Clean up Your Act Heads or Tails Money Talks Pick a Pocket Ready, Set, Drip!
Research	All That Glitters Is Not Gold Can You Put a Price on It? Get Rich Quick Money Research Shop 'Til You Drop Where Are the Federal Reserve Banks?

All Rights Reserved

Objective	Student Activity
Review	Warm-Ups Class Shop Money Games Problem Solving
Setting Goals	Contract All That Glitters Is Not Gold Shop 'Til You Drop
Sorting and Classifying	Warm-Ups Coupon Math Wishing on a Star
Time Management	Contract All That Glitters Is Not Gold Get Rich Quick
Use of Reference Material	All That Glitters Is Not Gold Money Research Where Are the Federal Reserve Banks?
Writing Skills	Warm-Ups All That Glitters Is Not Gold It Pays to Advertise Money Mania Writing About Money
Visual Discrimination	Warm-Ups Coin Rubbings Heads or Tails

TEN STEPS
TO SUCCESS

Ten Steps to Success

Step One

Know the Skills You Want Learned

Most school curriculum guides identify a hierarchy of skills for learning about money:

1. identifying coins

2. counting coins to $1.00

3. finding the fewest coins to make a certain amount

4. counting coins over $1.00

5. making change

6. _____

7. _____

8. _____

9. _____

10. _____

For more Details, Details, Details on how these "basic" skills will impact your success with this unit, refer to Being Prepared, page 86.

©1995 ECS Learning Systems, Inc.

Step Two

Make Your Classroom Teach

For students to independently use the project activities, and to provide you with time to teach to individual needs, you will need to create seven areas in your classroom:

1. Class Shop
2. Science Table
3. Research Shelf
4. Art Corner
5. Computer Shelf
6. Game/Supply Area
7. Small Group Learning Area

Since the supplies and areas needed in your classroom depend on the activities you choose for the money unit, use the chart on the following pages to select activities that will meet the needs of your students. Note: Some activities require materials other than a pencil. The chart lists materials needed, as well as specific directions for some activities.

After selecting the appropriate activities for your class, use page 41 to make a personalized table of contents. (This will be used as a checklist during the project.) Then, copy a Student Activity Packet for each student. This will consist of the cover page, table of contents, contract, Warm-Up 1, Warm-Up 2, and the activities you have selected.

For Details, Details, Details on setting up the seven learning areas in your classroom, as well as software, game, and book suggestions, refer to Being Prepared, page 87.

✔ *TRIED AND TRUE*
A successful interactive classroom has everything labeled, everything!

Student Activity Information

Activity	Target Subject	Special Notes
Warm-Ups	Pre-Assessment	
All Change!	Math (computation, problem solving)	For younger students, a collection of real coins is beneficial so they can manipulate the coins and count to find the solutions. This activity can also be done with no additional props, if the student mentally figures the solutions.
All That Glitters Is Not Gold	Social Studies	Students will need reference books, atlas, and paper.
Can You Put a Price on It?	Social Studies	
Cheap! Cheaper! Cheapest!	Math (percentages)	Students will need a calculator.
Class Shop	Drama Play Math	It is beneficial to have as elaborate a shop as you can put together, with shelves, a counter, and a cash register. However, a small shop is better than nothing! The students can bring in a variety of product boxes to display. You should label each item with a price within the range of numbers you would expect your students to be able to add. You can assign higher prices for more difficult shopping problems, and adjust the prices on the shopping cards accordingly. Students will also need money—real money is best! Finally, students will need shopping cards. These are cards with specific instructions written on them telling the student what to purchase at the class shop. Page 18 has examples of shopping cards. These, along with any cards you create, may be glued on index cards and laminated.
Clean Up Your Act	Science	Students will need dull pennies, small paper cups, lemon juice, clock or other timer.
Coin Rubbings	Art	Students will need a penny, nickel, dime, quarter, half dollar, and a soft pencil.
Collect a Dollar	Math (computation)	Students will need a die, $3 in various coins, and a partner.
Coupon Math	Math (computation, problem solving)	Students will need a wide variety of "cents-off" coupons.
Design a Fast Food Park	Math (computation, problem solving)	Students will need colored pencils, markers, or crayons.
Forgery!	Art	Students will need colored pencils, markers, or crayons.
Get Rich Quick	Art/Craft	The supplies students will need will vary; usually paper and art/craft supplies.
Heads or Tails	Math (graphing, probability)	Each student will need one coin.
Inflation!	Math (addition)	Each student needs two sheets of money playing cards. The students cut out the cards and write their initials on the back so the cards can be stored and returned to the owner at the end of each game. **How to Play:** 2-6 players. Players have their cards face down in front of them. All players turn over one card simultaneously, and total the coins shown on their own card. They announce their total and the person with the highest total wins all the cards displayed in that round. In the case of a tie, the students involved each turn over another card and total it. The highest total wins all cards that have been exposed in that round. The game is played for a predetermined amount of time. The player with the most cards is the winner. Or, the player who collects all the cards wins. (This is very difficult and takes a long time.) At the end of a game, the cards are returned to their owners and placed in the storage envelope on the Inflation! activity page.

Student Activity Information

Activity	Target Subject	Special Notes
It's in the Bag	Art/Craft	Students will need crayons or markers.
It Pays to Advertise	Language Arts	Students will need newspapers, magazines, and crayons or markers.
Making Faces	Art Math (computation)	Students will need colored pencils, markers, or crayons.
Money Games	Math (computation)	Students will need a minimum of two commercially made (e.g., *Monopoly*) or teacher-made games.
Money Mania	Language Arts	
Money Research	Social Studies	Students will need encyclopedias or other reference books pertaining to countries.
Money Talks	Math (graphing)	
Papier-Mâché Bank	Art	Students will need diluted white glue or wallpaper paste, strips of newspaper, strips of tissue, balloons, "junk" such as cardboard toilet tissue and paper towel rolls. **Directions:** Cover an inflated balloon with strips of newspaper that have been coated with paste. Overlap the strips and continue gluing until the balloon is covered. Next, cover the balloon with strips of tissue. Continue covering the balloon this way until there are three layers of newspaper and three of tissue. Use the "junk" in between layers to give the shape of legs and a nose. Let the balloon dry between layers. Cut a money slit in the bank and remove the balloon. Decorate the bank carefully and creatively.
Pick a Pocket	Math (graphing)	Students will need graph paper and a volunteer.
Problem Solving	Math	
Ready, Set, Drip!	Science	This activity is best set up in a science area, but can be done at the student's desk. Students will need water, eye droppers, paper towels, and a magnifying glass (optional).
Shop 'Til You Drop	Social Studies	
Take a Handful	Math (computation, problem solving)	Students will need a bag or tub full of various coins.
Where Are the Federal Reserve Banks?	Social Studies	Students will need an atlas. Teacher's Key: 1. Boston 7. Chicago 2. New York 8. St. Louis 3. Philadelphia 9. Minneapolis 4. Cleveland 10. Kansas City 5. Richmond 11. Dallas 6. Atlanta 12. San Francisco
Wishing on a Star	Math (computation)	Students will need magazines, catalogs, glue, and scissors.
Writing About Money	Language Arts	Students will need paper for a rough draft.

Shopping Cards

Cut out these instructions and glue onto index cards. Laminate if desired.

What can you buy with 53¢?	Buy something that grows above ground and pay with the exact money.
But something that is not a food. Give the exact change.	Buy two items that total less than 94¢.
Can you buy four items and spend less than 56¢?	Buy something that costs less than 15¢ and something that costs more than 30¢. How much did you give and how much did you get?
Buy three things for dinner that total less than $1.64. Explain what you got and the cost.	Buy two things without sugar that total less than 44¢.
Buy something that is eaten raw and something that is eaten cooked.	How many things can you buy with 38¢?
How many things can you buy with 69¢?	What can you buy with 17¢?
Buy three things you really like. How much did you spend? Did you pay with the exact change?	What items can you buy for $2.55?
If you bought a snack and gave 90¢, how much change would you get?	If you bought things for a picnic, how much would you spend?

Step Three

Communicate with Home

"Be Prepared" is a great motto, not only for boy scouts, but also for teachers!

As you know, a lesson can sink or swim depending on the time spent planning it. We want this money unit to not only swim but fly! So, be generous with the time you invest before you actually begin the classroom work. The greatest investment you can make is with your students' parents.

A class newsletter or other home communication is essential to the success of this money unit. Here are a few ideas to include in your communication with parents:

- Explain that an exciting integrated unit will be coming up in the near future.
- Drop a few hints about this innovative teaching method.
- Tell what a wonderful learning experience this will be.
- Explain that the study will cover curricular areas other than math.
- Give a taste of what is in the Student Activity Packet.
- Ask parents for their help with the new project. Tell them that they could contribute to the unit's success by coming and talking to the class about their money experiences. They could share the experiences of a banker or store keeper, demonstrate balancing a checkbook, or share a coin collection—anything that could be tied to money.

Take the time to communicate with your students' parents, and they will be your strongest allies and best advocates.

The note on the next page should be sent home the week before the unit starts, following the home communication that tells of the project, explains the rationale, and asks for volunteer "money" speakers. This will equip your classroom with plenty of real money to learn with.

For more Details, Details, Details on how to involve parents and get their support for this money unit, refer to Being Prepared, page 96.

All Rights Reserved   19

Dear Parents,

As you know, we will be starting our money unit very soon. It is extremely beneficial for the students to work with real coins. Therefore, I would like each student to bring the following coins:

    25 pennies
    10 nickels
    10 dimes
    5 quarters

The coins will be pooled in a class money box, so we will have real coins to use in a variety of math situations. Following our unit, the money will be put toward a class field trip.

Thank you!

Sincerely,

_____

20

Step Four

Ten Steps to Success

Set the Stage for Learning

To prepare your students for the money unit, you must do the following:

1. Create a money mind set.
2. Give an overview of the entire project.
3. Let the students browse through the Student Activity Packets.
4. Work on the Warm-Ups in the Student Activity Packet as a whole class and share the results together.

For Details, Details, Details on introducing this money unit to your students (as well as some fun classroom money ideas), refer to Being Prepared, page 97.

Step Five

The Contract and Checklist

Note: The contract and table of contents/checklist in the Student Activity Packet will be used for this step.

Prior to discussing contracts with the students, you have some decisions to make:

- How many activities are you going to require the students to complete in class? (Some activities that are not completed in school can be given as homework assignments.)
- Which activities will be mandatory?
- What is your time frame for the unit?

For Details, Details, Details on the responsibility lesson, refer to Time Management and Work Evaluation, page 99.

When you have your plan of action, it is time for the first lesson in the money unit—and the theme of the lesson is **responsibility**. There are five elements to this lesson:

1. Indicate the time frame.
2. Identify mandatory activities.
3. Have students choose from remaining activities.
4. Have students mark activities on the table of contents/checklist.
5. Have students complete the work contract.

©1995 ECS Learning Systems, Inc.

Step Six

Check in with Your Students

Needless to say, most children will not "magically" become self-directed learners just because they have directions and a contract. Just as it is important to inform the children what you will be doing while they are working, it is equally important (for your peace of mind) to know what they are doing. Since no teacher can be aware of every student during every work session, we would like to share the next best thing, the quick class check-in. Feel free to use the form provided on page 24 to keep track of individual progress.

✔ *TRIED AND TRUE*
Begin each work session with a quick class check-in.

For Details, Details, Details on how the quick class check-in can keep you informed on everyone's progress, refer to Time Management and Work Evaluation, page 100.

Quick Class Check-In

Student's Name	What activity are you doing first?	How many activities have you completed?	Questions*	Questions*

*Write in your own questions.

Step Seven

Work and Behavior Rubrics

We will define rubric the way we would for the students: A rubric is a tool used to measure how well you are (or are not) meeting class expectations.

Money Unit Work Rubric

"Not good enough" work is...
- not following activity directions
- handwriting that is sloppy and hard to read
- sentences that are incomplete

"Just right" work is...
- following most of the activity directions
- handwriting that is sometimes hard to read
- sentences that are sometimes incomplete

"Excellent" work is...
- following all directions for all activities
- all handwriting is neat and easy to read
- all sentences are complete with capitals and periods

Money Unit Behavior Rubric

"Not good enough" behavior is...
- speaking in a loud, distracting voice
- moving too quickly around the room
- not returning materials after using them

"Just right" behavior is...
- speaking in a low voice most of the time
- walking from activity to activity most of the time
- returning most of the materials after using them

"Excellent" behavior is...
- speaking quietly with others all the time
- walking carefully around the room all the time
- returning all materials after using them

✔ **TRIED AND TRUE**
Many schools and programs provide pre-written rubrics (like these) for teachers and students to use, but we have found that the most effective and meaningful rubrics have been the ones that children have helped us write.

For Details, Details, Details on how to write rubrics with your students, refer to Time Management and Work Evaluation, page 100.

Ten Steps
to Success

Step Eight

Discover the Learning Canyon

The "learning canyon" is the distance between what a child knows and what a child needs to know. There are three types of assessment used to discover and bridge the learning canyon.

1. Tests

Pre- and post-tests for both achievement and attitude have been provided. These tests will show you where the canyons are for each child and how well (s)he has crossed them.

The achievement test (pages 27-30) is designed to expose your students to every part of the money curriculum (different grade levels will focus on different areas). As a pretest, the achievement test allows you to know where each of your students is so you can begin to form small instructional groups based on exactly what students need. Some children will need more direct instruction than others; however, all children will be taught just what they need. The included Money Skills Checklist (page 31) can be used to manage the individual skills for each child.

The attitude survey (page 32) will give you a glimpse into students' attitudes toward math. Also given as a pre- and post-test, this survey will demonstrate any changes in students' attitudes and motivation due to their experience with this money unit.

The results of the test and survey are valuable indicators of the money unit's success with children.

2. Quick Assessments

These take place during small group instruction and let you know how well the child is crossing the canyon (see Step Nine).

3. Performance Assessments

Also included are two performance assessments (pages 33 and 34) to be managed by the students in the class shop. You have the option of using these "real life" assessments to show what your students have learned.

©1995 ECS Learning Systems, Inc.

Achievement Test

Name_____ Date_____

1. Write the name of each coin and its amount:

_____   _____   _____

_____¢   _____¢   _____¢

_____   _____

_____¢   _____¢

2. Write the total amount these coins are worth.

   _____¢

3. You have $1.00. You are going shopping. You buy a candy bar for 35¢ and a gum ball for 15¢. How much change do you get back?

_____¢

4. You are going shopping for suckers. You want to buy four. They cost 30¢ each. You have $1.00. How much more money do you need?

_____¢

5. Write the total amount these coins are worth.

_____¢

Write about the fastest way to count these coins.

_____

_____

_____

6. You have $5.00. You go out to lunch and buy a hamburger for $1.95, fries for $.95, and a soft drink for $.50. How much change will you get back?

$_____

7. Draw and label the fewest coins to make the following amounts.

27¢

_____

72¢

_____

96¢

Tell me everything you know about MONEY.

_____

_____

_____

_____

_____

_____

_____

_____

_____

_____

_____

_____

_____

_____

©1995 ECS Learning Systems, Inc.

Money Skills Checklist

Student's Name	Coin ID	Count Coins up to $1.00	Make Change up to $1.00	Count Coins over $1.00	Make Change over $1.00	Fewest Coins

All Rights Reserved

Please carefully read the statements below. Answer TRUE or FALSE after each statement.

I like math.

_____

Math is fun.

_____

I know a lot about math.

_____

I like math better when I get
to choose my activities.

_____

I feel in control of learning math.

_____

I want to know more about
math.

_____

I learn better in small groups.

_____

I am smart in math.

_____

Math is one of my favorite
subjects.

_____

Math is easy for me.

_____

©1995 ECS Learning Systems, Inc.

Make a Purchase

Name _____ Date _____

Take a handful of coins.
Separate them into groups.
Name the groups.
Count the coins.
How much money do you have? _____
Visit the class shop and make a purchase.
Write about what you bought (name, cost, change).

_____

_____

_____

_____

_____

Did You...

	Yes	No
1. Make groups of coins?	____	____
2. Count the coins?	____	____
3. Buy something at the class shop?	____	____
4. Pay with the correct amount of money?	____	____
5. Use the fewest coins possible to pay?	____	____

All Rights Reserved

Making Change

Name _____ Date _____

Visit the class shop to sell something.
Collect money from a customer and count it.

How much? _____
Give the customer change for the purchase.

How much? _____
Use the fewest number of coins possible.
Count the change back to the customer.
Write about what was bought and the change you made (name the fewest coins).

_____

_____

_____

_____

_____

Did You...

	Yes	No
1. Count the money paid?	____	____
2. Give back change?	____	____
3. Use the smallest number of coins?	____	____
4. Count back the change?	____	____

©1995 ECS Learning Systems, Inc.

Step Nine

Ten Steps to Success

Bridge the Canyon

This is the point where assessment and instruction merge, and direct instruction and learning take place.

- Use your completed Money Skills Checklist from the achievement pretest.
- Form small, flexible ("flex") groups of students with common learning needs.
- Prepare your instructional material for each skill to be taught (worksheets, textbooks, manipulatives, etc.).
- Prepare a "quick assessment" for each skill you will teach in order to monitor individual learning progress.
- Use the "Flex" Groups Worksheet (page 36) to manage each of your small learning groups.
- Always follow up with your "flex" groups to check for retention.

For more Details, Details, Details on creating "flex" groups and quick assessments, refer to Assessment and Instruction, page 103.

"Flex" Groups Worksheet

★ = skill demonstrated   ✔ = skill NOT demonstrated

	Names	Skills Taught	Quick Assessment Results	Follow Up
Date ____				

	Names	Skills Taught	Quick Assessment Results	Follow Up
Date ____				

	Names	Skills Taught	Quick Assessment Results	Follow Up
Date ____				

©1995 ECS Learning Systems, Inc.

Step Ten

Ten Steps to Success

Let the Games Begin

By now you have accomplished the following:

- You know what skills you have to teach.
- You have the necessary supplies available and labeled in your classroom, and you have selected and copied the activities to fit the needs and abilities of your students.
- You have sent a letter to parents and collected real money.
- You have launched the project with a motivating activity and introduced the Student Activity Packet to your students.
- Your students have completed their work contracts.
- You are ready to check in with your students to hold them accountable.
- You have written work and behavior rubrics with your students, or you are using the ones provided.
- You know where the learning canyon is for each student.
- You have created small "flex" groups using the Money Skills Checklist, and you are ready to keep track of your work with each group using the "Flex" Groups Worksheet.

With all this in place, you are ready to turn the power switch ON for interactive, integrated, independent learning in your classroom.

Notes

STUDENT
ACTIVITY PACKET

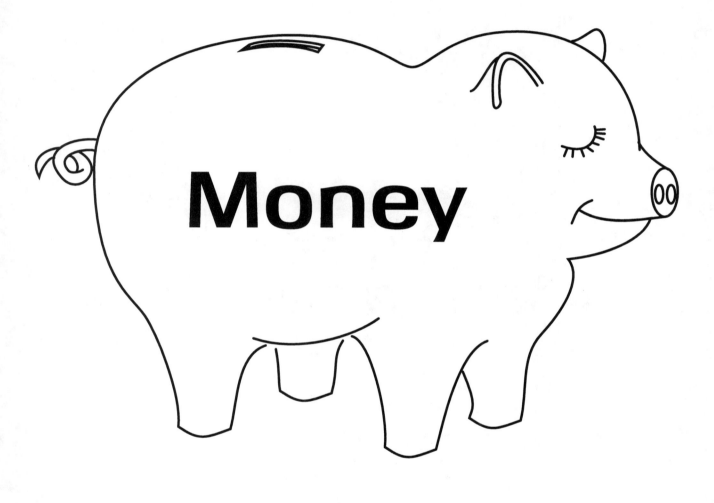

Money

Name _____

©1995 ECS Learning Systems, Inc.

Contents

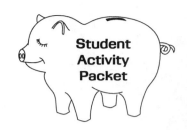

Student
Activity
Packet

Contract

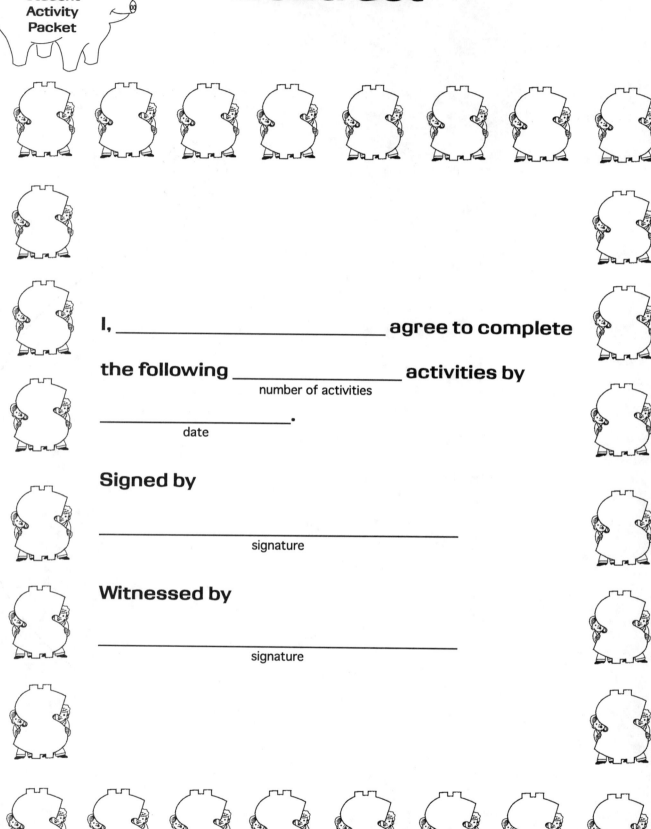

I, _____ agree to complete

the following _____ activities by
              number of activities

_____.
      date

Signed by

_____
              signature

Witnessed by

_____
              signature

Warm-Up 1

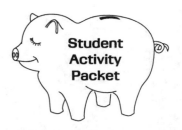

Examine a dime and a penny. Use the Venn diagram to record how they are alike and different.

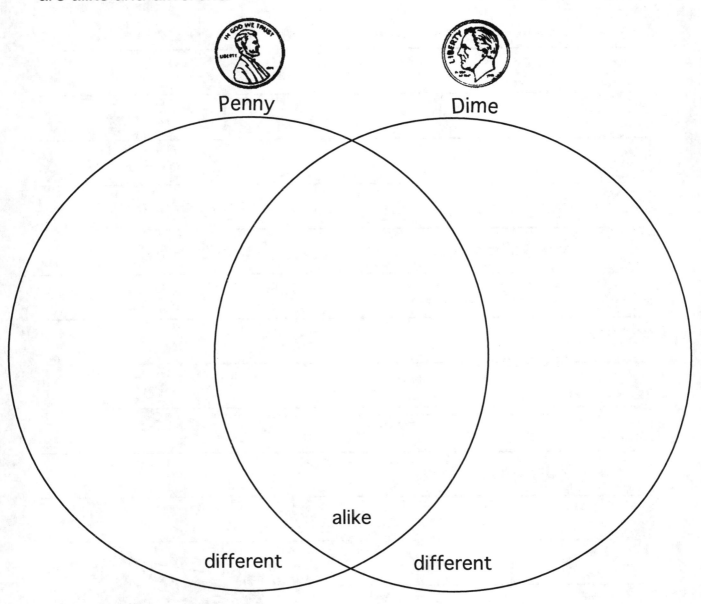

Penny

Dime

alike

different

different

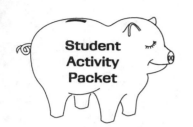

Warm-Up 2

Tell what you know about money. Write in sentences, giving as much detail as you can.

_____

_____

_____

_____

_____

_____

_____

_____

_____

_____

_____

_____

©1995 ECS Learning Systems, Inc.

All Change!

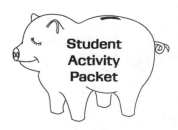

Make 50¢ using the number of coins stated. Draw the coins in each picture. Write P for penny, N for nickel, D for dime and Q for quarter on your coins.

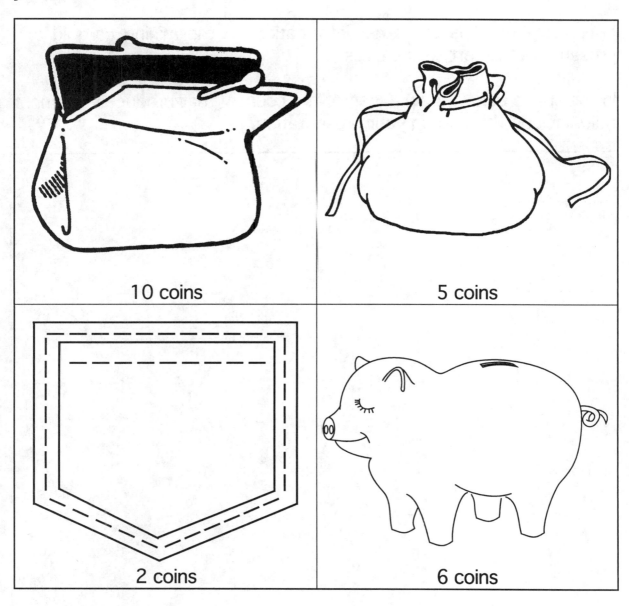

10 coins

5 coins

2 coins

6 coins

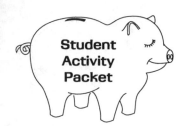

All That Glitters Is Not Gold

This is a research assignment, so be ready to do some detective work! As you know, gold is very important to the world economy, but what do you actually know about it?

Your assignment is to gather information on the mining of gold and present your report to the class.

In the space below, draw a map of the country that produces the most gold. Include this map in your presentation.

©1995 ECS Learning Systems, Inc.

Can You Put a Price on It?

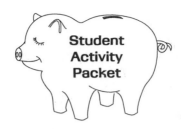
Student Activity Packet

You are going to find out what people consider **valuable** and what they consider **precious**. First you should be sure you know the meaning of those words. Take your survey to a busy area of the school. Stop people and ask them to tell you the most valuable item they have. Record their answer on the diagram. Then ask them to tell you the most precious thing they have, and record that answer, too. Can you figure out where to record the response, "My most valuable thing is my most precious thing too!"

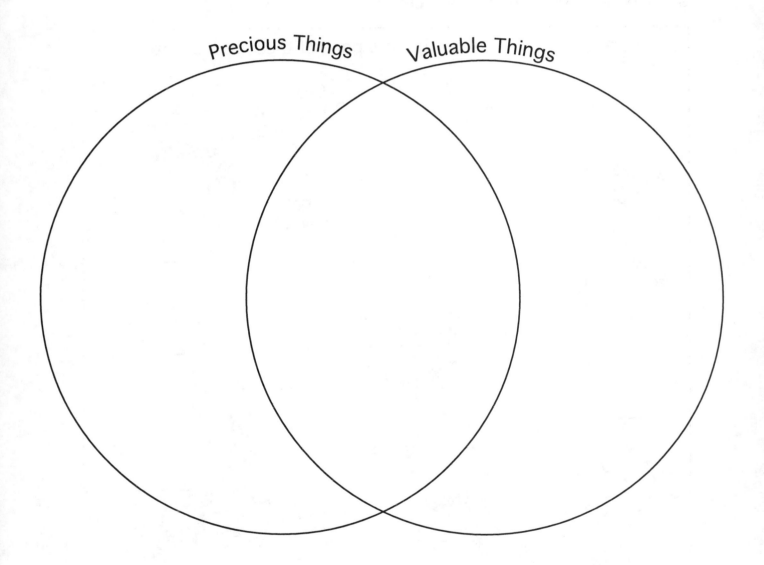

Precious Things

Valuable Things

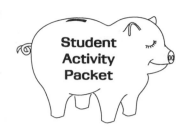
Cheap! Cheaper! Cheapest!

Smart shoppers look for sales, but what exactly does 50%, 10%, 33% mean in money? It is easy to find the sale price when you follow these calculator steps:

1. Enter the regular price.
2. Press subtract.
3. Enter the amount of discount, such as 50, 10, 33.
4. Enter %.
5. Round to the nearest cent.

Use these steps to calculate the new price of these reduced items.

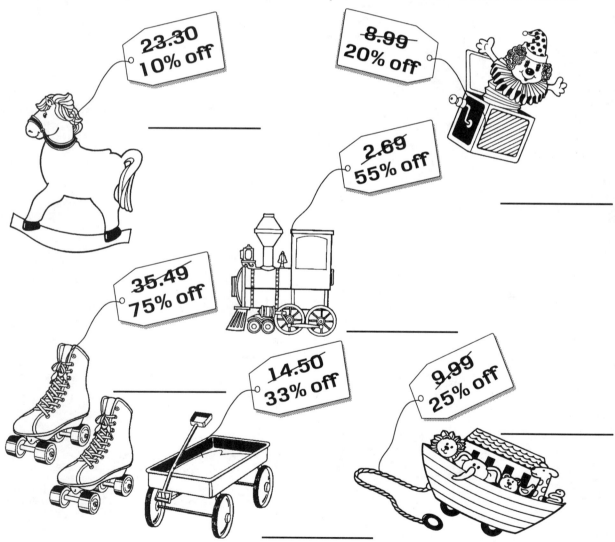

23.30
10% off

8.99
20% off

2.69
55% off

35.49
75% off

14.50
33% off

9.99
25% off

48   ©1995 ECS Learning Systems, Inc.   All Rights Reserved

Class Shop

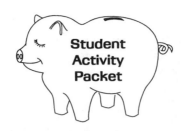

Play in the class shop. You can be a shopper or a salesperson. Use shopping cards. Choose your two favorite cards to record here.

Copy your shopping card here, and then write what you did to complete the task.

Copy your shopping card here, and then write what you did to complete the task.

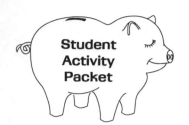

Clean Up Your Act

Place some dull pennies in a cup and cover them with lemon juice. Leave them for about five minutes.

Draw your experiment. Describe what happened and hypothesize (guess!) why it happened.

_____

_____

_____

_____

_____

_____

©1995 ECS Learning Systems, Inc.

Coin Rubbings

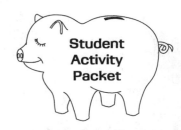

Use a pencil to make rubbings of a penny, nickel, dime, quarter, and half dollar.

	Heads	Tails
Penny		
Nickel		
Dime		
Quarter		
Half Dollar		

Make a rubbing of the coins that would total 27¢.

Collect a Dollar

Make your own money game. The object of the game is to be the first to collect a dollar. To make the game, write directions in every third square. Some should bring the player money, such as "It is your birthday, collect 10¢ from the bank." Some should cost money, such as "You are late for school, pay the bank an 8¢ fine." To play the game you need a friend, a die, a game board, and approximately $3 in coins for the bank. Decide on the rules with your friend.

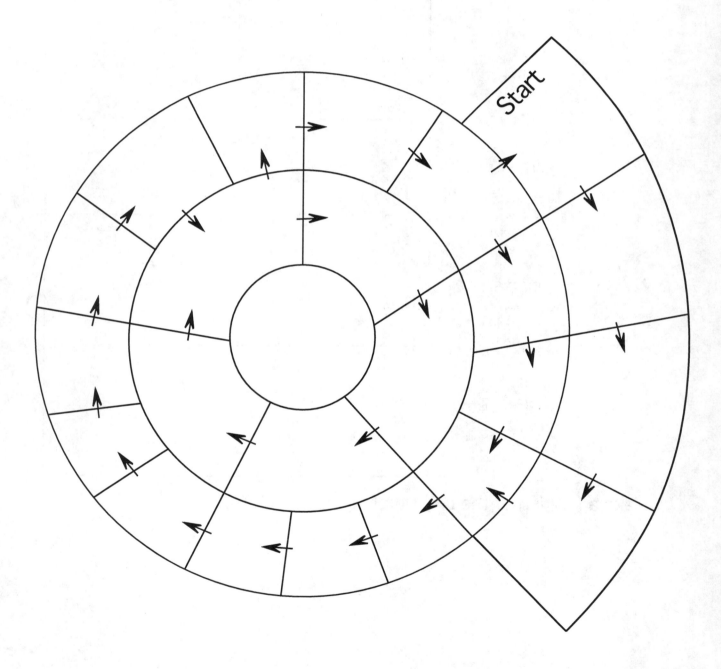

Coupon Math

Student
Activity
Packet

Use six "cents-off" coupons to do the following activities.

1. Arrange the coupons in order from least valuable to most valuable.
    Write the amounts here.

    _____

    _____

2. Arrange the coupons in order of expiration date. Write the dates here.

    _____

    _____

3. Arrange the coupons in order of what you like best to what you like
    least. Write them here.

    _____

    _____

4. Figure out the total value of your coupons if you could get cash for
    them.

    TOTAL _____

5. Divide your coupons into two piles: odd cents amounts and even cents amounts.

    How many coupons are in each pile? _____ odd _____ even

    Find the average amount of each pile. _____ odd _____ even

6. Divide the coupons into two piles: necessities and luxuries. Be ready to explain why you sorted them that way.

7. Use a "sticky note"—or paper clip and paper—to attach the following information to each coupon:

    > the length and width of the sides
    > the area and perimeter of the coupon

Keep your coupons clipped to this page when you are not using them.

Design a Fast Food Park

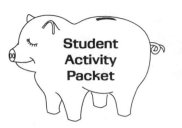

Design a park for a fast food restaurant. The restaurant is free, but you must pay for everything else. Here is the price list:

Parking lot	$ 10
Lake	$ 1
Tree	$ 1
Bench	$ 2
Slide	$ 12
Swing set	$ 5
Merry-go-round	$ 18
Picnic table	$ 3
Bridge	$ 16
Petting zoo	$ 25
Animals	$ 10 each
Swimming pool	$ 35
Water slide	$ 10

Your piece of land has a stream and three trees. Design your park any way you want to, but don't spend more than $100. Draw your plan on the map on the next page.

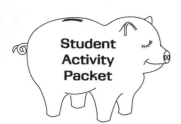

My Fast Food Park

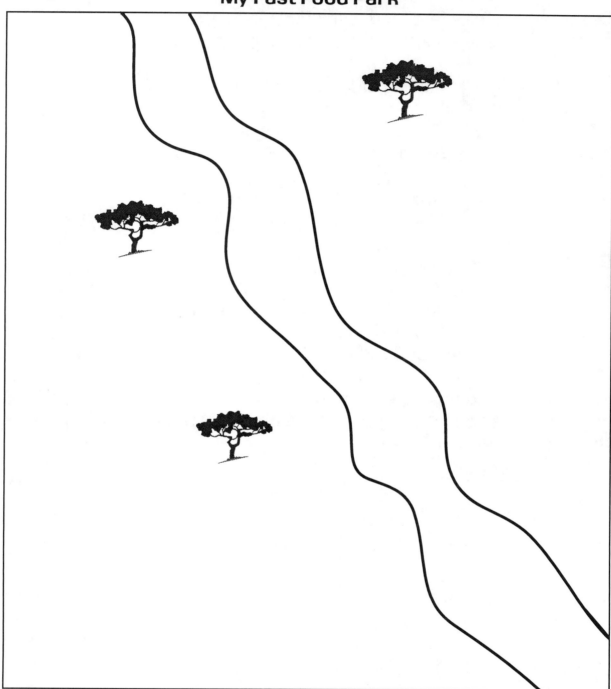

Total cost $_____

Amount left out of $100 $_____

         ©1995 ECS Learning Systems, Inc.

Forgery!

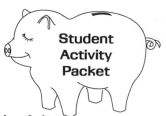

Design your own coins and bank notes. Be creative and colorful!

heads

tails

front

back

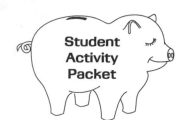

Student
Activity
Packet

Get Rich Quick

This activity challenges your creativity. You are going to make something that your classmates will want to buy with class money. Brainstorm a list of possible products, and then do a survey to see if there is an interest in any of them. The list has been started for you. Don't rush into this project. Put some effort into your market research and it will pay off for you.

Item	Consumer Interest?
bookmark	
tissue flowers	
drawings	

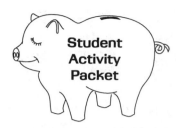

Be sure to keep account of your costs, and the number of items sold. Subtract the cost of your supplies from the money you made. This will give you your profit.

Supplies

Item	Amount
Total Amount	

Sales

Customer	Amount
Total Amount	

Total Amount Sold – Total Amount of Supplies = Profit

_____ – _____ = _____

Heads or Tails

You are going to flip a coin 40 times and record how many times it lands heads up and how many times it lands tails up. After each flip, color in a box to show if your coin was heads or tails. Predict the result. How accurate was your prediction?

Predict first!

How many heads?

_____

tails?

_____

Were you accurate?

yes   no

(circle one)

Heads

Tails

©1995 ECS Learning Systems, Inc.

Inflation!

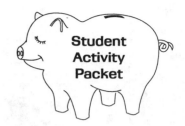

Cut out the money cards on the next two pages and find some friends to play the game with you.

If your cards are the same color as your friends' cards, make sure you have your initials on the back of your cards so you can get them back when the game is over.

To Play: Place your cards face down in a pile in front of you. All players turn up one card from their pile at the same time. Add up the amount of money shown on your card and announce it to your friends. The player who has the highest amount wins all the cards played in that round. The cards are placed at the bottom of the winning player's deck, and the game continues.

To Win: 1) Win all the cards.
                        or
              2) Have the most cards when time is called.

GOOD LUCK!!
Keep your cards in here for future use.

Glue an envelope here.

MONEY CARDS

©1995 ECS Learning Systems, Inc.

M O N E Y   C A R D S

It's in the Bag

In the space below, design a paper bag that could be used in the class shop.

When you are happy with your design, get some paper and make a full-size sample of your bag. You can use it when you shop, or display it on the wall.

©1995 ECS Learning Systems, Inc.

It Pays
to Advertise

Look at advertisements in newspapers and magazines. Make a list of the words they use, and how they are written.

Sale   **Buy Now!**   **BARGAINS**

REDUCED

_____

_____

_____

_____

Design an advertisement for a product of your choice in the space below.

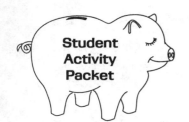

Making Faces

Draw five different faces on the following page, using the noses, mouths, and eyes shown. Figure out the cost of each face.

NOSES

        35¢   17¢   7¢

MOUTHS

        6¢   25¢   52¢

EYES

        15¢   45¢   22¢

#1

_____

#2

_____

#3

_____

#4

_____

#5

_____

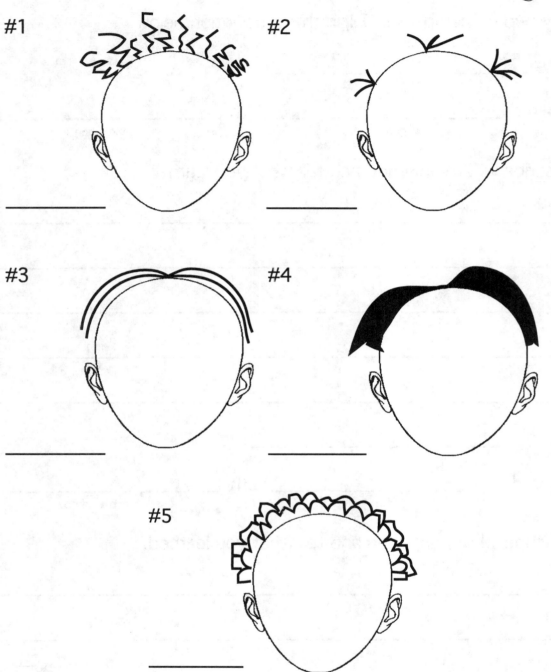

Your cheapest face is # _____

Your most expensive face is # _____

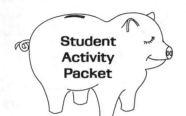

Money Games

Play two money games. Fill in the information below.

1 Date _____

I played _____ with _____ .
game   friend's name

Describe what happened and tell what you learned.

_____

_____

_____

_____

_____

2 Date _____

I played _____ with _____ .
game   friend's name

Describe what happened and tell what you learned.

_____

_____

_____

_____

Money Mania

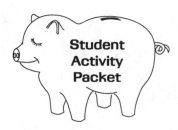

Ask a friend for the nouns, verbs, and adjectives to fill in the blanks. Don't let your friend see the page. Read the hilarious paragraph to your friend after the blanks are filled in.

One day _____ and _____ went to the mall to shop
            name   name

for _____. They had been saving their _____ and they
    plural noun   plural noun

had a total of _____ _____. The first store they came
         number   plural noun

to sold _____, but they already had enough of those. The
      plural noun

next store sold _____ and they needed _____ of
          plural noun   number

those, so they _____ in. They spent $_____
          verb   number

and _____ cents. They gave the clerk _____
     number   number

_____ and got _____ _____ in change. Lots
  plural noun   number   plural noun

of the _____ were having sales so they spent all their_____.
    plural noun   plural noun

They bought a _____ _____, _____ _____,
      adjective   noun   adjective   noun

_____ _____, _____ _____. Tired
  adjective   noun   adjective   noun

and _____, they bought _____ _____.
    adjective   number   plural noun

They _____ in their _____ and went home.
   past tense verb   noun

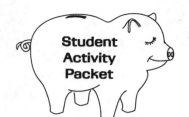

Money Research

Make the longest list you can of countries and the money they use. The "effort meter" will keep track of how much your effort is worth!

Here are some to start you off!

Effort Meter	Country	Currency
1¢	• England • Canada • Mexico	Pound Dollar Peso
5¢	• • •	
10¢	• • •	
25¢	• • •	
50¢	• • •	
$1	• • •	

©1995 ECS Learning Systems, Inc.

Money Talks

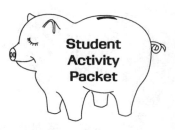

Have you ever wondered how your allowance compares with that of other kids? Well, this is your chance to find out! Survey kids at your grade level, and record your data on the bar graph below.

The Allowance Graph

#of Students										
more than 10										
9										
8										
7										
6										
5										
4										
3										
2										
1										
	less than $1	$1-$2	$2-$3	$3-$4	$4-$5	$5-$6	$6-$7	$7-$8	$8-$9	more than $10

Weekly Allowance

What conclusions can you draw from your allowance graph?

_____

_____

_____

_____

_____

_____

_____

_____

_____

_____

_____

_____

©1995 ECS Learning Systems, Inc.

Papier-Mâché Bank

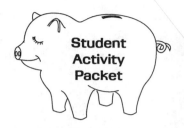

Make the weirdest, wildest bank creature you can for saving your money! Before you begin to make your bank, look at the materials you will be using and plan what your bank will look like. Draw your bank below. When you have made your bank, compare it to the plan you drew.

To make your bank, you will need:

- diluted white glue or wallpaper paste
- strips of newspaper
- strips of tissue
- an inflated balloon
- "junk," such as small boxes and cardboard paper towel rolls, for legs and a nose

Cover an inflated balloon with strips of newspaper that have been coated with paste. Overlap the strips and continue gluing until the balloon is covered. Next, cover the balloon with strips of tissue. Continue covering the balloon this way until there are three layers of newspaper and three of tissue. Use your "junk" in between layers to give the shape of legs and a nose. Let the balloon dry in between layers. Cut a money slit in the bank and remove the balloon. Decorate your bank carefully and creatively.

Pick a Pocket

Find a person in the school who usually carries money, and ask if (s)he would be willing to help you with a money graph. You are going to graph the coins the person carries and find out which coin (s)he has most often.

Ask your volunteer to empty his/her pockets or purse. Sort the coins. Fill in the following information.

# of Pennies   _____   # of Nickels   _____

# of Dimes   _____   # of Quarters   _____

# of Half Dollars   _____   # of Dollar Coins   _____

Take the information back to class and record your data on the bar graph below.

Coins Carried by _____

	1	2	3	4	5	6	7	8	9	10	11	12	13	14	15	16	more
Pennies																	
Nickels																	
Dimes																	
Quarters																	
Half Dollars																	
Dollar Coins																	

Do the same each day for one week, using graph paper to record your data. At the end of one week, examine your graphs. What can you conclude from the data you collected?

_____

_____

_____

_____

_____

_____

_____

_____

_____

_____

_____

_____

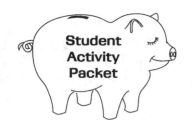

Student
Activity
Packet

Problem Solving

Are you money-wise? Test your skill by solving these problems.

1. You want some oranges. One store has them on sale for 8¢ each, and another store is selling them 10 for $1. Which is the better buy, and why?

    _____

    _____

    _____

2. You are at the movies. You pay $4.50 for your ticket, $1.50 for a drink, and 75¢ for popcorn.

    How much did you spend? $_____

    How much change would you get out of $10? $_____

3. Use the alphabet values to answer the questions on the following page.

A	B	C	D	E	F	G	H	I	J	K	L	M
$1	$2	$3	$4	$5	$6	$7	$8	$9	$10	$11	$12	$13

N	O	P	Q	R	S	T	U	V	W	X	Y	Z
$14	$15	$16	$17	$18	$19	$20	$21	$22	$23	$24	$25	$26

©1995 ECS Learning Systems, Inc.

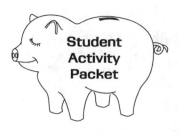

How much is your name worth? $_____

Which of your friends' names is worth the most? Write the name and the value.

_____
name

$_____
value

4. If girls are worth five nickels each and boys are worth two dimes and five pennies each, what is the value of the students in your class?

$_____

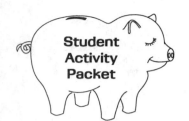

Student Activity Packet

Ready, Set, Drip!

How many drops of water can you fit on a coin? Try this experiment and record your results. Remember, always predict first!

	Prediction	Result
Number of drops on a penny		
Number of drops on a nickel		
Number of drops on a dime		

Describe what you did and what happened. Explain why the experiment worked the way it did.

_____

_____

_____

_____

_____

_____

_____

Shop 'Til
You Drop

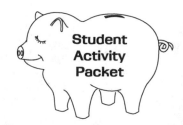

This activity has two parts, one to do at school and a follow-up activity for home.

Part One

You need to plan a healthy, balanced meal for your family. If you are not sure what foods are needed for a healthy, balanced meal, you need to research this before you do the activity. Using your best estimate, fill in the chart below.

Healthy Meal Estimate

Food	Cost	Cost Per Serving*

*Divide the cost by the number of people you will be serving.

Part Two

Take the "Shop' Til You Drop" worksheets home and explain your assignment to your parents. Follow the directions on the next page.

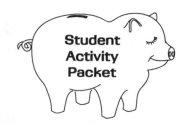

Copy the food items you have chosen in Part One onto the menu. Take this paper to the store and find the prices of the items on your menu. (Maybe you can actually buy them and fix a meal for your family!) Fill in the actual cost of your food items and calculate the actual cost per serving. Compare your results with your estimates in Part One.

Healthy Meal Menu

Food	Cost	Cost Per Serving*

*Divide the cost by the number of people you will be serving.

80   ©1995 ECS Learning Systems, Inc.

Take a Handful

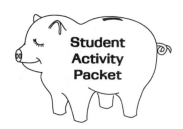

Take a handful of coins, then answer the following questions.

1. How many pennies did you pick? _____

   What is their value? _____

2. How many nickels did you pick? _____

   What is their value? _____

3. How many dimes did you pick? _____

   What is their value? _____

4. How many quarters did you pick? _____

   What is their value? _____

5. Use the coins to find the value of:

   three dimes and two nickels _____

   two quarters and three pennies _____

   four nickels and 12 pennies _____

6. Fill in the blanks.

   40 pennies is the same as _____

   one quarter is the same as _____

   two dimes is the same as _____

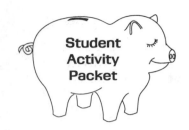

Where Are the Federal Reserve Banks?

Draw a line from the name to its location on the map.

1. B_____   2. N _____ Y _____

3. P _____   4. C _____

5. R _____   6. A _____

7. C _____   8. S___ L_____

9. M_____   10. K_____ C_____

11. D_____   12. S_____F_____

Use an atlas to figure out which of the Federal Reserve Banks is closest to you, and what the actual distance is.

Wishing on a Star

Find five things, in a catalog, that you would really like to have. Cut them out and glue them in your bag. What is the total cost of the items?

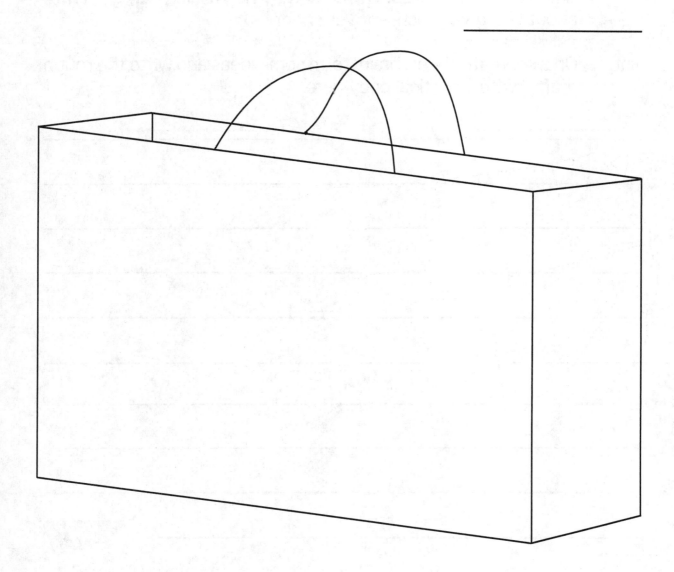

Challenge question:
If your allowance were three dollars a week, how long would it take you to save enough money to buy these items?

Student
Activity
Packet

Writing About Money

Write a poem or story about money.

Ideas: Pretend you are a penny and describe your adventures from the
time you were minted. Write about "The Wishing Penny." Write
about being very rich—or very poor.

Hint: On a separate sheet, brainstorm some ideas and write the rough
draft. Write your final copy here.

_____

_____

_____

_____

_____

_____

_____

_____

_____

_____

DETAILS,
DETAILS,
DETAILS

Being Prepared

Preparing Yourself

We are held accountable for teaching, and we hold students accountable for learning certain skills. The specific skills we teach are determined not by which grade we teach, but by what our students need to learn.

It has been said that within a single grade level there is an ability span of four grade levels. Textbooks do not address this situation, nor do whole-class math lessons. Even when children are grouped according to skill level and change classrooms for math, every student does not possess the same skills. Each student has an individual need that must be met. Busy work (worksheets and practice packets) never seems to keep the class busy enough for the teacher to work with a single student or a small group. Worse yet, busy work and textbooks do nothing to engage students and "turn them on" to math.

It has also been said that half the challenge in math is fostering a positive attitude toward it. This is true not only for the students, but for the teachers and parents as well. Most of us did not have an overall positive experience in math as we went through school; however, many of us are still teaching math the same way it was taught to us.

Starting with the skills that you know will need to be taught, let's move on to see how your classroom will be used to assist you in teaching these skills to your students.

©1995 ECS Learning Systems, Inc.

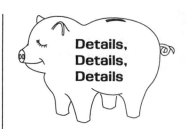

Preparing Your Classroom

A teacher's classroom is one of the most underutilized instructional tools in education. Whether your room has desks, tables, couches, pillows, or centers, you can transform your classroom into an interactive learning environment by paying close attention to how space is used in your room. With you and your classroom teaching at the same time, your students will be surrounded with opportunities to learn.

1. The Class Shop

This will be the most active area of your room, as well as the most permanent of all areas needed. It will also be by far the most popular. Choose a place in your room that will accommodate up to five students, a sales counter (a narrow table, a desk, or a cardboard box), and a merchandise display area (a bookshelf, a window sill, or another desk). Part of the fun of creating a class shop is deciding on a theme. Students can be involved in its creation (grocery store, fast food restaurant, toy store, etc.). After you provide the space, your students, or parent volunteers, can decorate and provide the supplies necessary for the shop to operate. Here are some ideas we have used:

- Grocery Store—The students brought empty food boxes and cans, and together we labeled the items with appropriate prices for the students' age (35 cents, 45 cents, etc.).
- Fast Food Restaurant—Using donated wrappers, cups, and bags from our local fast food restaurant, we set up a mock restaurant where students ordered from a menu and then recycled their orders back to the supply shelf.

The ideas for the class shop are nearly endless, and the "real life" experience adapted to the classroom gives students an opportunity to use money in a "real" way.

To focus the use of this area, and avoid the "What do I do?" question, there is a set of shopping cards on page 18. You may use the cards provided or personalize shopping cards for your class shop. Remember to label your shop for easy identification. Your students can make a sign as they help design the shop.

Details, Details, Details

2. The Science Table

Integrating hands-on science into your math curriculum can be difficult, but the benefits far outweigh any extra effort it will require. Your students will independently practice the scientific process:

- identifying a problem
- hypothesizing a solution
- experimenting
- observing the results

A sign outlining the steps in the scientific process would be helpful to direct your students through the science experience.

The space needed to carry out the science experiments is minimal. You may want to provide a separate area for up to five students to work, or you can simply provide the supplies. Students can easily perform the experiments at their desks.

3. The Research Shelf

Most classrooms already have access to research materials such as encyclopedias and nonfiction books. For the "Money Research" activity it is important to make resources available that will identify the currency in a variety of countries. This is an excellent way for students to practice using an index to find specific information. An old (or new, if you are fortunate) set of encyclopedias is essential for an interactive classroom; however, if encyclopedias are not available, collect as many nonfiction books on various countries as you can from your local or school library. An attractive sign should be made to direct your students to this area.

The following list suggests additional books on the subject of money that you may want to include in your classroom during your money unit.

Nonfiction

Everything You Need to Survive Money Problems by Jane and Jovial Bob Stine, Random House, New York, 1983. Students get advice on making, saving, and spending money with a few jokes and games in between. Intermediate.

Fast Cash for Kids by Bonnie Drew, Homeland Publications, Seabrook, TX, 1987. Money-making projects for kids to do. Primary/intermediate.

From Barter to Gold: The Story of Money by Solveig Paulson Russell, Rand McNally, San Francisco, 1961. The history of money for kids. Primary/intermediate.

Good Cents: Every Kid's Guide to Making Money by Amazing Life Games, Houghton, 1974. A collection of ideas for making money and doing creative things with it (besides spending it). Intermediate.

If You Made a Million by David Schwarz, Lothrop, Lee and Shepard Books, New York, 1989. Sure to be a class favorite! Watch money grow from a penny to a million bucks. Checking accounts and interest are made clear for all readers. All ages.

Kids' Money Making Environmental Jobs by Jodi Jill, Kid's Environmental Publishing House, Boulder, CO, 1992. Kids' jobs that provide money while sharing the responsibility of cleaning our environment. All ages.

Making Cents: Every Kid's Guide to Money by Elizabeth Wilkinson, Little, Brown and Company, Boston, 1989. Everything any kid ever wanted to know about money. All ages.

Math Fun with Money Puzzlers by Rose Wyler and Mary Elting, Julian Messner, New York, 1992. A challenging collection of problem solving activities for teachers to use with students or students to use themselves. Primary/intermediate.

The Monster Money Book by Loreen Leedy, Holiday House, New York, 1992. This picture book follows monsters as they learn how to count money, purchase items, and use a bank. Primary.

Round and Round the Money Goes by Melvin and Gilda Berger, Ideal Children's Books, Nashville, TN, 1993. An excellent reading book for primary children that explores money around the world, banks, and more. Primary.

The Story of Money by Betsy Maestro, Clarion Books, New York, 1993. An excellent read-aloud book, packed full of fun facts. All ages.

Toothpaste Millionaire by Jean Merrill, Houghton Mifflin, Boston, 1972. Learn how a kid made over a million dollars by selling a better and cheaper toothpaste. Primary/intermediate.

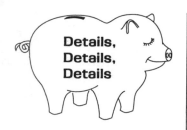

Details, Details, Details

Understanding Money; What Is Money?; Managing Your Money by Elizabeth James and Carol Barkin, Raintree Editions, Milwaukee, WI, 1977. Good information about coins, checking and savings accounts, and credit cards. All ages.

What to Do When Your Mom or Dad Says, "We Can't Afford It!" by Joy Wilt Berry, Living Skills Books, Fallbrook, CA, 1983. A book for kids about a real kid problem. Primary/intermediate.

Fiction

Alexander, Who Used to Be Rich Last Sunday by Judith Viorst, Atheneum, New York, 1978. Watch Alexander lose his money as he realizes all the things a dollar can do. Primary.

Arthur's Funny Money by Lillian Hoban, Harper, New York, 1990. Arthur goes into business with Violet to make money. Primary.

The Berenstain Bears' Trouble with Money by Stan and Jan Berenstain, Random House Publications, New York, 1983. This story follows the Berenstain Bear family in their adventure with money. Primary.

Business Is Looking Up by Barbara Aiello, Twenty-First Century Books, Fredrick, MD, 1988. When a blind child starts a business, he discovers that there is more to it than just making money. Primary/intermediate.

Dollars and Cents for Harriet: A Money Concept Book by Betsy and Giulio Maestro, Crown Publishers, New York, 1988. Learn about how coins add up to a dollar as readers follow Harriet in her attempt to buy a new kite. Primary.

Get Rich Mitch! by Marjorie Weinman Sharmat, Morrow, New York, 1985. After winning a sweepstakes, Mitch becomes a celebrity and learns how life changes. Intermediate.

Jason and the Money Tree by Sonia Levitin, Harcourt Brace Jovanovich, New York, 1974. Follow Jason in his fantastic adventure when he plants a money tree. Intermediate.

Million Dollar Jeans by Ron Roy, Dutton, New York, 1983. Tommy finds and then loses a million dollar lottery ticket when his jeans are given away. Intermediate.

Pigs Will Be Pigs by Amy Axelrod, Four Winds Press, New York, 1994. Follow the pig family as they learn about money while looking for enough money to eat dinner out. Primary.

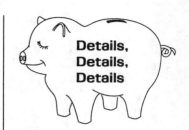

4. The Art Corner

Like the science table, this could be a space for up to five students to work together, or it could be a supply area for the students to work at their desks. Either way, by bringing art into the math curriculum, you will see students less anxious about what they are learning because they will be having fun while they learn.

The only supplies really needed for the "Coin Rubbings" and "Design a Dollar" activities are pencils and colors (markers, crayons, or colored pencils will do). This does not necessitate a large amount of space or clean-up.

The "Papier-Mâché Bank" project will require additional space, supplies, and clean-up. It may best be done as a whole-class activity.

A quality example of each activity gives students an expectation to strive toward. These examples can be created by you, a student, or a parent volunteer prior to the activity. A sign to draw attention to your quality examples will be a necessity for your art corner.

Details, Details, Details

5. The Computer Shelf

Depending on your available equipment, this area may or may not exist. A list of suggested educational software is provided below.

Apple

Market by Compuware, 1994. Produce, advertise, and price your own products to see who can make the most money. Ages 8 and up.

Marketplace by MECC, 1984. Manage a lemonade stand and try to make a profit. Ages 8 and up.

Moneyworks by MECC, 1987. Students participate in games that range from counting coins to making change to making their own money and spending it in different countries. Ages 6 and up.

Oregon Trail by MECC, 1985. Students must budget their survival as they cross the country by covered wagon. Ages 8 and up.

IBM

Monopoly by Virgin MasterTronic, Inc., 1989. The classic board game computerized. Ages 8 and up.

Spin for Money by Generic Computer Products, 1987. Players are rewarded with money during this word skill game. Ages 8 and up.

Apple/IBM

Free Enterprise by Science Research Associates. Teams of students engage in a business simulation where quarterly decisions are made. Ages 10 and up.

Treasure Math Storm by The Learning Company, 1994. Students must calm the storm on Treasure Mountain by reviewing basic math skills, including money skills. Ages 5 to 9.

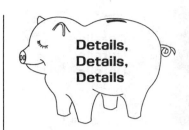

6. The Game/Supply Area

This is the final classroom space that your students will use independently. As with the art area, students will become engaged in these math games because they make learning fun. Again, you may want to provide a space for up to five students to make and play math games, or you may have them use the floor for this purpose. Playing games with other students at individual desks can be disruptive to those students who are working on an activity alone.

The more games you have available for your students, the better. A list of suggested money games is provided below.

Cityopoly Games by Cityopoly, 1989. These "Monopoly-like" games are personalized for your favorite city (like *Denveropoly*). Ages 8 to adult, 2 to 8 players.

Don't Go to Jail by Parker Brothers, 1991. A dice game based on *Monopoly*. Ages 8 to adult, 2 or more players.

Greed by The American Greed Co., 1987. A strategy dice game that tests the greed of all the players. Ages 7 to adult, 2 to 8 players.

Monopoly by Parker Brothers, 1985. The classic money game. Ages 8 to adult, 2 to 8 players.

Monopoly Junior by Parker Brothers, 1990. The classic money game for younger players. Ages 5 to 8, 2 to 4 players.

Presto Change-O by Educational Insights, 1992. Learn to make change by playing this award-winning game. Ages 5 to adult, 2 to 4 players or teams.

The following consumer math board games are by Creative Teaching Associates, Fresno, California, 1-800-767-4282.

Allowance, 1979. Earn and save money while making purchases. Grades 3-8, 2 or more players.

Bank Account, 1976. Students make "real-life" transactions including writing checks, making deposits, and keeping an accurate balance. Grades 5 and up, 2 or more players.

Budget, 1977. Experience "real-life" economics on a $2,000 budget. Grades 4 and up, 2 or more players.

Department Store Math, 1977. Purchases are made from a catalog while reference skills and change-making skills are practiced. Grades 4-8, 2 or more players.

Fun at the Fair, 1983. Players spend money and make change while going to the fair. Grades 2-6, 2 or more players.

Primary Money Chase, 1979. Practice money recognition and equivalencies. Grades K-3, 2 or more players.

Shopping Bag, 1975. Players make purchases in a grocery store using problem solving skills. There are four levels of difficulty. Grades 3-8, 2 or more players.

Details,
Details,
Details

7. The Small Group Learning Area

While the students are interacting with all the different activities in your classroom, you will be interacting with the students. You will be working with small groups of students on specific skills dictated by the curriculum and your students' needs.

It will be necessary to have a centrally located space to work with up to ten students. If there is not table space available, a floor area will work just fine (clipboards are an essential supply for floor instruction).

With an instructional area that is centrally located, you will also be aware of the interactions occurring around you, and the students who are making choices in the various areas will be aware of your presence.

Minimal adjustments made to any classroom can create an environment that teaches as much as you do. Once you and your room are ready, it is time to bring your students and their parents into the picture. How can you prepare them?

✔ *TRIED AND TRUE A "Do Not Disturb" sign is essential to motivate students to find their own solutions rather than interrupt your direct instruction.*

Details,
Details,
Details

Preparing Your Students and Their Parents

It pays to advertise. Invest heavily in your parent community, not just for your money unit, but from day one of the school year. By taking the time to advertise and explain yourself—your educational philosophy and teaching methods—you will prevent many common parent/teacher problems. By communicating regularly with the parents, you can educate them about teaching methods that are very different from when they went to school, and so avoid the confrontation that begins, "When I was in school…!" By communicating regularly with the parents, you can reassure them that their child is doing something valuable in class, and not "Nothing!"—which is the response elicited from the child whenever the anxious parent tries to find out what (s)he is doing in class!

Be proactive. You will feel as if you are in control, not just reacting to parental inquisitions. When parents see that you are open about the activities you plan, and that you are willing to explain what goes on in your room, they will relax and have more confidence in you. We have found that parents will support the most unconventional teaching methods if the teacher takes the time to explain the objectives and the reasons behind that particular approach. We have been able to teach innovatively and creatively in fairly conservative schools because we were proactive.

Communicating with parents is vital. If you can get the parents "on your side," school will be a more pleasant place for all concerned. Parents are not the enemy. Bear in mind, parents are highly invested in their child. They want the best possible education for their child, and it is important that you let them know their child will be getting that with you.

Details,
Details,
Details

Creating a Money Mind Set

You can create a money mind set in your students in a number of ways:

- Bring in your coin collection and talk about it.
- Read a book about money (see page 89 for suggested book titles).
- Watch a movie about money.
- Take a field trip to a bank, a U.S. Mint, a store, or other money-related place.
- Have a guest speaker who is involved with money (maybe a parent).
- Introduce the idea of class money as a reward (and punitive fines) system, and ask the students to submit their currency designs for the class to vote on.

In our classrooms, the class money was accumulated for an end-of-the month auction. The students could use their money—independently, or cooperatively in cartels (yes, they called them that, and understood the concept!)—to bid on small items, new or used, the parents had donated.

Whichever way you choose to introduce the topic, your enthusiasm will be picked up by the students. Enthusiastic learners are what we all strive for!

After the initial introduction of the topic, by whatever means you choose, explain the concept of interdisciplinary learning, employing user-friendly language, of course! You might want to illustrate the explanation with a web diagram and include examples from the Student Activity Packet (see example on page 98).

✔ *TRIED AND TRUE*
Class money has proven to be a very successful classroom management strategy, and a tremendous learning experience in money management!

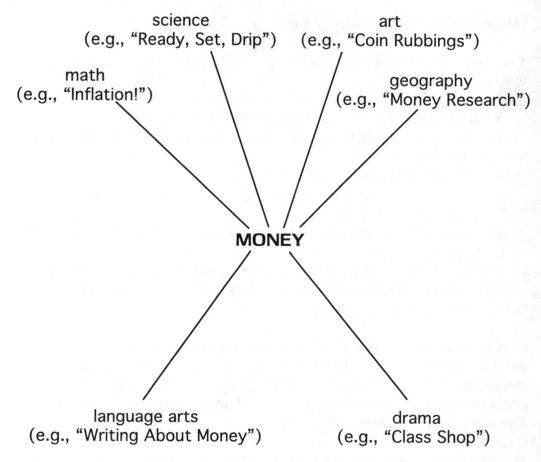

science
(e.g., "Ready, Set, Drip")

art
(e.g., "Coin Rubbings")

math
(e.g., "Inflation!")

geography
(e.g., "Money Research")

MONEY

language arts
(e.g., "Writing About Money")

drama
(e.g., "Class Shop")

After this, and preferably on another day so as not to overwhelm the students, hand out the Student Activity Packet for a browsing session. No activities should be done at this time. However, students can do the two Warm-Up activities and share the results with the class. Your aim is to give the students a taste of things to come, to fire their interest and enthusiasm, and to make them ready to learn!

At this point, your students and their parents should be well prepared and eager to plunge into the money unit with enthusiasm and commitment!

Time Management and Work Evaluation

Details,
Details,
Details

Lesson #1 — Responsibility

Tell the students which activities in the Student Activity Packet are required by you, and have them mark these on the contents page, which doubles as a checklist. It is a good idea to have a uniform way of indicating required activities, to prevent any confusion. Once you have told your students which activities are mandatory, explain the time line for all the work—so they don't panic and think this all has to be done by the end of the day.

Explain to the students that they are in the fortunate position of having some control over their learning, but with that control comes responsibility. They will be required to sign a contract which states they promise to complete a certain number of activities which includes those they may select themselves, as well as those activities required by you.

Emphasize that students should select their activities thoughtfully because once they have agreed to do certain activities, they are bound by the contract to complete them. Perhaps a breach of contract fine—paid with class money, of course (see page 97 for a description of class money)—would lend a little seriousness to the contract. Explain the concept to the students and let them decide on the punitive consequences for those who fail to live up to their obligations!

When this has been decided, allow the students time to discuss the activities with one another and reach a decision on which activities they are willing to commit to. Have the students select, then mark, the activities they have chosen.

Now it is time to fill in the contract. This should be done very seriously so the students know it is an important undertaking. It is beneficial to let the students work in pairs at this time, one witnessing while the other completes and signs the contract, and then switching roles.

The contract signing should conclude the money unit for this period. It brings closure to the lesson and leaves the students with a sense of anticipation for the next work period, when they will actually begin work in their Student Activity Packet.

Details, Details, Details

Quick Class Check-In

A quick class check-in is a management and accountability tool that will take five minutes at the most. Begin by reminding the whole class of the work and behavior expectations for the project (via the rubrics), then choose a question of the day to ask each child publicly. You might ask any or all of the following questions during the course of the project:

- What activity are you doing first today?
- How many activities have you completed?
- How many activities did you do yesterday?
- How many activities do you have to do to complete your contract?

These questions focus the students and give you information on their progress. If you start with "What are you doing first?" you will be able to tell if an activity is overcrowded. To do this quick class check-in publicly also gives you a verbal commitment from each child to do a certain activity that day. It is a good idea to let each child proceed to the selected activity after checking in with you. This prevents a swarm of children moving all at once.

Writing Rubrics Together

We like to ask students the following question: If school were like a basketball, soccer, or football game, could you play without knowing the rules? After receiving a resounding "no" or "not very well," we explain that just like there are rules for sports that you are expected to follow in order to win, there are expectations (rules) in school that you need to know in order to win. The expectations for this money unit need to be stated for the students so they can know how they are doing in behavior and work.

We have written rubrics with students for many activities from handwriting to keeping a room clean, and the results have always been the same. When the children knew exactly what was expected, they performed to exceed that expectation. Here's how it works.

Decide on a label for each of three levels of expectation. Here are some examples:

- low, average, high (This labeling is rather boring.)
- basic, proficient, advanced (This is what we use.)
- not good enough, just right, excellent (This is a little spicier.)

The words you choose are not as important as the attitude that accompanies them. Almost all children want to be high, advanced, or excellent.

Set the "proficient" expectation. For your grade level and your group of children, your expectations for work and behavior must be very specific and observable. For example, in third grade three "proficient" behavior expectations would be:

- Speak in a low voice when asking a question or sharing information with someone else.
- Walk around the classroom when you change activities.
- Return all materials after using them.

Three "proficient" work expectations would be:

- Follow all directions for each activity.
- All handwriting must be neat and easily read.
- All written work must contain complete sentences.

Brainstorm, with the whole class, descriptions for a "basic" and an "advanced" expectation for each of your "proficient" expectations. For example, your students may decide that an "advanced" descriptor for the "All written work must contain complete sentences" expectation would be "All written work must be in paragraph form and contain five sentences each." The "basic" descriptor could be "All written work is not in sentences." The students have fun setting the standards for high and low achievement while at the same time internalizing the expectations.

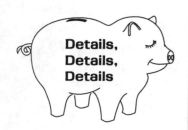

Details, Details, Details

After all the descriptors for behavior and work expectations have been made, assign some students to make a large poster with each rubric on it for easy viewing.

Begin each work session by reviewing the rubrics prior to the quick class check-in. You may even want to ask each student where (s)he would rate him/herself on each rubric before setting out to work.

After the "rules of the game" have been made and posted, the students begin to ask questions like, "Does this look proficient or advanced?" and "What do I need to do to make this excellent?" As a teacher, you can use the rubrics to give specific direction to the children during this money unit. You can say things like, "Your voice is basic right now. What can you do to change that?" and "It is wonderful to see so many advanced workers in this room!"

With such clear, internalized expectations, daily work accountability, and a contractual commitment, you and your class are well on your way to making the impossible dream of having self-directing, managing, and evaluating students very possible.

©1995 ECS Learning Systems, Inc.

Assessment and Instruction

Moving from Point A to Point B

Once you have organized your teaching classroom and your students are independently involved with the activities, the direct assessment and instruction begins.

Since children come to school with varied money experiences, it is essential to discover what they know and don't know so direct skills instruction can take place. The distance between what a child knows and what a child needs to know is like a canyon. Our job is to figure out where the canyon is and choose the best way to cross it. During this time of high accountability in education, it is important to be able to offer "proof" to parents and administrators that learning is taking place in your classroom. This is where pre- and post-tests and checklists become valuable communication tools. The information you collect on your checklist will also be used to create your small "flex" groups.

Compared to the more traditional way of grouping students in math, where they took a test at the beginning of the year and were "stuck" in high, average, and low groups for the remainder of the year, the idea of creating small "flex" groups will either sound like a dream come true or an organizational nightmare.

It is not a nightmare! Small "flex" groups allow you to teach quickly and specifically to the academic needs of each student in your class. However, you must use the skills checklist to keep track of what has been learned and what needs to be taught for each student.

After discovering the learning canyons for each child, gather together a small group of children (ten at the most) with the same academic need. These groups are called "flex" groups because they must be flexible, allowing a child to flow in and out as the need arises. Use a quick assessment to discover what aspect of the skill each child needs to learn. An example of a quick assessment for coin identification would be simply showing the child a coin and asking what it is called and how much it is worth. Record the results of the quick assessment for each child and then **teach** what they need to know. Feel free to use textbooks or additional worksheets to reinforce and provide practice with the new skills.

103

**Details,
Details,
Details**

A quick assessment is a very specific performance assessment using real objects. The same quick assessment can be used to see if the child has bridged the learning canyon. After bridging successfully, that small group dissolves and new groups with new academic needs form. When all the students have successfully mastered the expected skills, the learning canyon no longer exists, and the project can come to an end.

Before you embark on a journey across the learning canyon, remember these six points:

1. Discover the canyon (pretest).
2. Record academic needs on the skills checklist.
3. Create small "flex" groups.
4. Quickly assess skills to discover specific needs.
5. Teach and give opportunity to practice.
6. Prove that you have crossed the canyon (post-test).

If you felt that assessment and instruction were tied together as we addressed the issue of the learning canyon, then you are correct. Assessment and instruction are the hand rails used for keeping you on the bridge as you cross the canyon.

Problems That Arise

Details,
Details,
Details

We hope you have found the process of preparing to use the money unit in your classroom smooth and organized; however, we all know that life isn't always smooth or organized, especially with a wide diversity of students in a classroom. There are four types of students you may encounter during the project that could pose a challenge to its success. We would like to introduce you to these students ahead of time, as well as provide some suggestions for dealing with them so you can be prepared for the inevitable.

The "What Do I Do Now?" Student

This is the student who has difficulty making choices independently, and seems to need the teacher to direct his every move. This student needs to learn to become self-directed, but not by sapping your time from other students. This student needs to specify two or three activities that he will work on each day. As he commits to them, ask him which he will do first, second, and third. At the end of the work time, check in with this student on his progress.

The "This is Too Hard/Easy" Student

This student is either in need of a challenge or a simpler approach to the activity. Teach this student that she can change the numbers to make them larger or smaller depending on her needs. She may also be a candidate for an independent money study. She could decide with you the limits and expectations for the study. The following are some suggestions:

- How is money made?
- How does a bank work?
- Research a U.S. President on a favorite coin.
- How can a kid set up a savings account?
- Plan a meal using $10.00 (use prices from newspaper).
- What is the stock market?

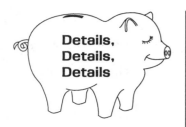

The "All Talk, No Action" Student

This student takes advantage of the interactive environment to further his own social life instead of working. This student can be very sneaky and look like he is doing what he should, but one glance at his activity book proves otherwise. After referring to the behavior rubric, he can be easily dealt with by controlling where he works and how he works. Sit this child near you without any contact with other students for a day. More often than not, he will decide it is preferable to keep his social life outside of your work time.

The "Messy, Messy, Messy" Student

This student lacks care in the neatness of her work. First refer to the rubric, then say three words: "Do it over!" Most of the time she will have figured it out by remembering the rubric that she helped write.

We are sure that these problems will not affect most of your students because you have involved them in the learning process. That in itself takes care of most problems.

©1995 ECS Learning Systems, Inc.

The End...
And Then Some

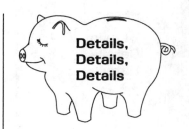

Details,
Details,
Details

As you know, educators are faced with increasing challenges in today's classroom. The project approach to teaching and learning, advocated in this book, helps teachers meet—and conquer!—those challenges.

This money unit is very structured and controlled, although the student is given much greater freedom than is usually allowed in a more traditional teaching situation. This is a great way to introduce interdisciplinary learning and project work.

Students who learn through projects will:

- learn basic skills in a holistic, meaningful way
- work in small groups or one-on-one with the teacher
- learn time management and natural consequences
- feel some control and ownership and, therefore, commitment to the work
- learn how to assess the quality of their work through rubrics
- learn the basics of research in several curriculum areas
- gain experience in compiling and delivering oral, visual, and written presentations
- experience an excitement about their school work
- feel control over their learning
- be involved, committed, and invested in the project

Hopefully, this has been a good experience for the teacher, too! Project work enables teachers to:

- adopt an interdisciplinary approach to teaching
- promote independent learning
- assess students through valid tasks
- structure learning so the needs of both the high and low functioning students are met
- devise a valid grading/evaluation system
- create a stimulating environment
- foster a love for, and an excitement about, learning

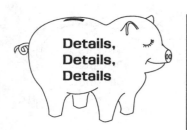

Details, Details, Details

Good books on teaching through project or topic work are still quite hard to find, but one that should not be missed is *Engaging Children's Minds: The Project Approach* by L. Katz & S. Chard (Ablex Publishing Corp., 1989). This integrated approach to teaching has been used, with much success, in England for many years. Here are two excellent books on project work from England:

Project Teaching by David Wray (Scholastic Publications Ltd., 1988)

Developing Topic Work in the Primary School edited by C. S. Tann (Falmer Press, 1988)

These books will guide you through your first independent project, and give you the confidence you need to be successful.

When you embark on project work, remember that it is not done in addition to the regular curriculum work. You plan for the project to encompass a variety of curricular subjects and enrich the students' knowledge, stretching them to explore a topic beyond usual curricular boundaries. Your knowledge of curriculum expectations is vital. You should be so familiar with what you are expected to teach that you never miss a chance to fit a requirement into what you and the students really want to do. If you are expected to teach the use of capital letters, do it during a project; likewise with grammar, punctuation, etc. Instead of teaching isolated skills, you can make this "mundane" learning relevant and meaningful by incorporating it into project work.

You did it! It worked! Why stop now?

Be brave! Be innovative! Be successful! It is very scary letting go of traditional teaching. There is always someone ready to warn you that "If you give them an inch, they'll take a mile!" That first step toward giving students some control over what they do in the classroom is a step into the great unknown!

Feedback, Please!

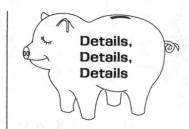

Details,
Details,
Details

On the following pages there are two response sheets—one for the students and one for you—that are essential to the improvement and success of our future interactive, integrated learning projects. Please share your experience as a teacher with us. The student form is equally important and can be reported by tallying the whole-class results on one form. Please send both response sheets to us, as we are constantly seeking to provide better educational experiences for students and teachers.

Thank You!

Please send completed forms to:

Todd Daubert and Pauline Nelson
c/o ECS Learning Systems, Inc.
P.O. Box 791437
San Antonio, TX 78279-1437

Student Evaluation Form

What did you think of the money unit? Answer YES or NO to each of the following questions.

Did you like math before the money unit?   _____

Did you feel in charge of your own learning during the money unit?   _____

Did the money unit make you want to learn more about money?   _____

Did you look forward to math time during the money unit?   _____

Did you like math better during the money unit?   _____

Would you like to learn math this way again?   _____

Did the money unit make you feel smart in math?   _____

Were the activities in the money unit fun?   _____

Did you feel like you learned a lot from the money unit?   _____

The best part of the money unit was:

_____

_____

Teacher Evaluation Form

Please rate each of the following statements.

		strongly disagree	disagree	no opinion	agree	strongly agree
1.	The Ten Steps to Success prepared me to use the money unit.	SD	D	NO	A	SA
2.	The Details, Details, Details section was useful.	SD	D	NO	A	SA
3.	It was easy making my classroom teach.	SD	D	NO	A	SA
4.	The student activities allowed my students to work independently.	SD	D	NO	A	SA
5.	My students were able to manage their time.	SD	D	NO	A	SA
6.	My small "flex" groups worked well.	SD	D	NO	A	SA
7.	My assessment of each student's needs was accurate.	SD	D	NO	A	SA
8.	My students' acheivement tests improved from the pretest to the post-test.	SD	D	NO	A	SA
9.	My students' attitude surveys showed improvement from pretest to the post-test.	SD	D	NO	A	SA

10. What do you see as the greatest strength and the greatest weakness in this way of teaching?

Strength _____

Weakness _____

All Rights Reserved

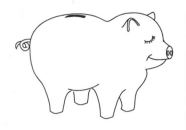

About the Authors

Todd Daubert received his training at the University of Denver. He recently completed his master's degree in curriculum and instruction at Colorado Christian University. He currently teaches in the Cherry Creek School District, Colorado.

Pauline Nelson has been a teacher for "twenty-something" years. She is English, and received her training and creative approach to education in England. She currently teaches in the Cherry Creek School District, Colorado.